How to use this book

This Year 2 Handwriting workbook is matched to the National Curriculum and is designed to improve handwriting skills.

Activities split into three levels of difficulty – **Challenge 1**, **Challenge 2** and **Challenge 3** – to help progression.

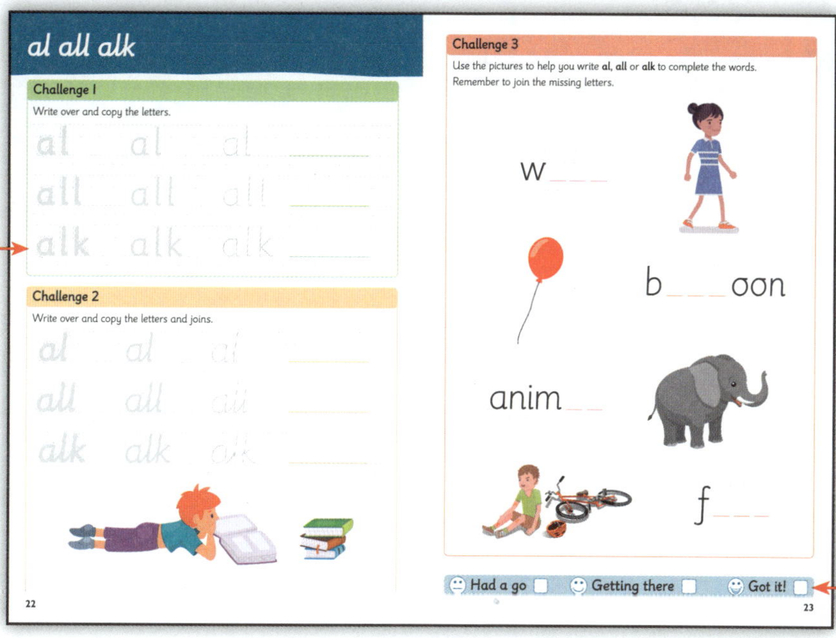

Opportunities for **self-evaluation** are included throughout.

Starter check recaps skills already learned.

Four **Progress checks** included throughout the book for ongoing assessment and monitoring progress.

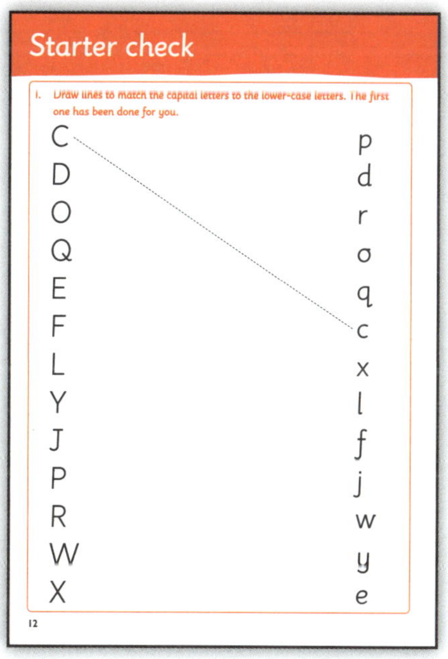

Contents

ACKNOWLEDGEMENTS

Published by Collins
An imprint of HarperCollins*Publishers* Ltd
1 London Bridge Street
London SE1 9GF

HarperCollins*Publishers*
Macken House
39/40 Mayor Street Upper
Dublin 1
D01 C9W8
Ireland

ISBN 978-0-00-853465-3

First published 2023

10 9 8 7 6 5 4 3 2

British Library Cataloguing in Publication Data.

A CIP record of this book is available from the British Library.

Publishers: Fiona McGlade and Jennifer Hall
Author: Chris Whitney
Series Editor: Dr Jane Medwell

Project Management and Editorial: Chantal Addy
Cover Design: Sarah Duxbury
Inside Concept Design: Ian Wrigley
Typesetting and Artwork: Jouve India Private Limited
Production: Emma Wood
Printed by Martins the Printers

FSC www.fsc.org MIX Paper | Supporting responsible forestry FSC™ C007454

This book is produced from independently certified FSC™ paper to ensure responsible forest management.

For more information visit: www.harpercollins.co.uk/green

Guidance for parents

Handwriting at home – Year 2

Parental support can make a huge difference to a child's handwriting development. Handwriting is the basis of complex literacy skills; a child who can write letters automatically can attend to all those other tricky aspects of writing — getting ideas, putting them in order, spelling, etc.

There are five very clear priorities for your child in relation to handwriting in Year 2:

- form lower-case and capital letters at the right size relative to one another
- correctly use diagonal and horizontal strokes needed to join letters
- understand which letters, when adjacent to one another, are best left unjoined
- use spacing between words that reflects the size of the letters
- use the names and alphabetical order of the letters in the alphabet to order items.

The first section of this workbook focuses on revising the correct movements to form letters, as this is the basis for correct joining and fluent handwriting.

This workbook gives your child practice of the five main types of joins between letters:

1. Diagonal joins to letters without ascenders (for example: *ai*)
2. Diagonal joins to letters with ascenders (for example: *ch*)
3. Horizontal joins to letters without ascenders (for example: *wa*)
4. Horizontal joins to letters with ascenders (for example: *wh*)
5. Joins to round (anti-clockwise) letters (for example: *ad*).

The focus of Year 2 is joining the letters using these joins and establishing good spacing and proportions.

The workbook also includes practice of capital letters, number formation and alphabetical order. Encourage your child to say the name of the letter whenever you can, as this will be useful in their spelling.

Holding a writing tool

A young child's pencil grip will gradually develop from a simple palmar grip (a fist) to the point where they can hold the pencil in three or four fingers and, eventually, hold the pencil between the thumb and index finger with the pencil supported on the middle finger.

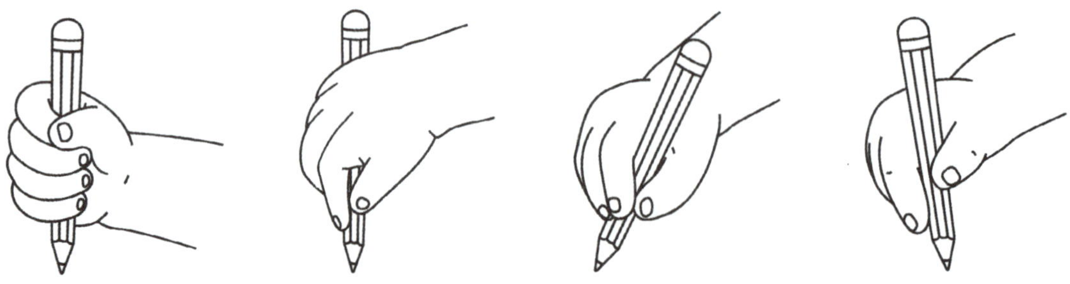

Stage 1: palmar | **Stage 2:** all fingers | **Stage 3:** three–four fingers | **Stage 4:** supported on middle finger

Show your child how you hold a pencil and help them to get better at it gradually. Aim for your child to have control of the writing tool but not to grip it too hard, as this will tire their hands and arms.

We recommend using a pencil for handwriting practice, because a plain lead pencil has a good combination of grip and slip. But if your child prefers colours or pens, why not? Make sure your child does not feel pressured to use a pen, simply because it is more adult — let them use whatever is most comfortable.

Left-handed children

Although most children are right-handed, around 10 percent of any population is left-handed.

Left-handed children may like to sit on slightly higher chairs and hold the pencil slightly further from the point to cope with the demands of letters designed for right-handers.

Letter formation

The priority in your child's early handwriting is to form each letter correctly, starting at the right point. Children who can do this will be able to write letters effortlessly and join them up in due course. If your child tries to start letters in the wrong place, gently redirect them to the correct starting point for the letter. Year 2 is a good time to check letter formation and practise correct formation of any letters your child is not sure about.

This workbook uses letter formations which are easy for children to do correctly and lead effortlessly into joined writing. On pages 6 and 7, you can see all the letters with arrows to show how they are formed and where each letter starts. The printed letters have exit strokes (flicks) which help when children start to join the letters. If children learn these letter formations, they will be able to learn letter joins with little effort.

Most Year 2 children will now form letters correctly. Encourage your child to position the letters on the line with regular spaces between the letters. Guide your child to make capital letters taller than lower-case letters.

Practising handwriting with your child

With practice, young children quickly learn to "feel" the correct letter movement or join, to develop fluent and even handwriting. We recommend doing frequent short practice sessions of 5–10 minutes in Year 2. Though this does not sound like very much, a few minutes a day really can make a positive difference.

When your child uses this workbook for handwriting practice, they will probably slant the page. Left-handers usually slant the top of the page to the right and right-handers slant the top of the page to the left. This is good practice. If your child can sit at a table to write, it will help them get used to doing this.

Self-evaluation

Talking with your child about their handwriting practice is very helpful. The "evaluation strips" at the end of every double page in this workbook allow your child to estimate their own progress. The "self-evaluation grids" in the "progress checks" are designed for you to discuss your child's progress at handwriting. The "progress chart" on the last page allows your child to record how they feel about their handwriting after completing the workbook. It is always good to notice and praise efforts or improvements as it helps your child become confident and proud of their handwriting.

Letter formations

Lower-case letter formations

a b c d e

f g h i j k

l m n o p

q r s t u

v w x y z

Capital letter formations

A B C D E

F G H I J K

L M N O P

Q R S T U

V W X Y Z

Warm up and revise

Write over and copy the letters.

c a d e s

f g o q

Find and circle the letters **c**, **a**, **d**, **e**, **s**, **f**, **g**, **o** and **q** in the words below.

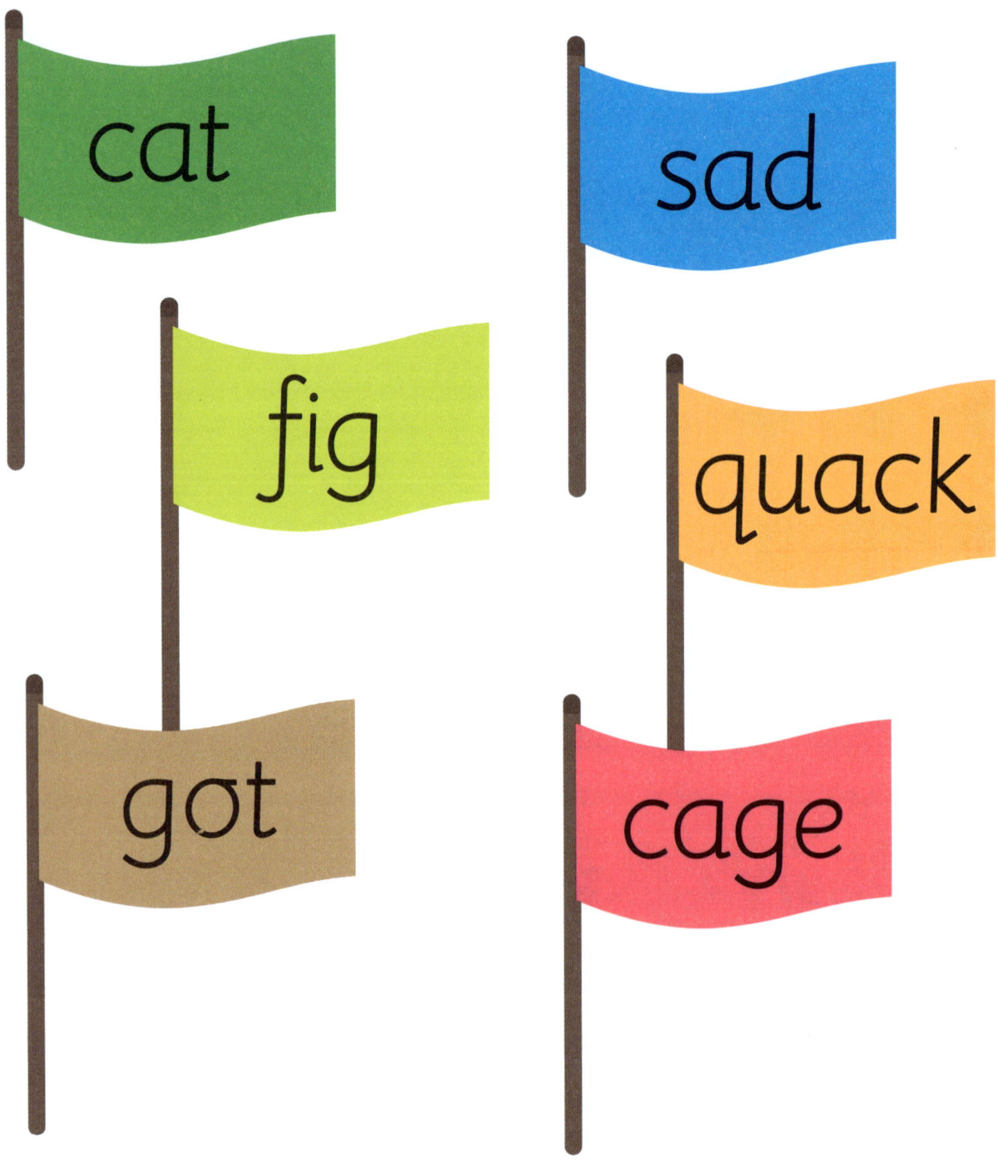

Write over and copy the letters.

i l t u

y j k

Find and circle the letters **i**, **l**, **t**, **u**, **y**, **j** and **k** in the words below.

Warm up and revise

Write over and copy the letters.

r n m

h b p

Find and circle the letters **r**, **n**, **m**, **h**, **b** and **p** in the words below.

pan 

nut 

shell 

map 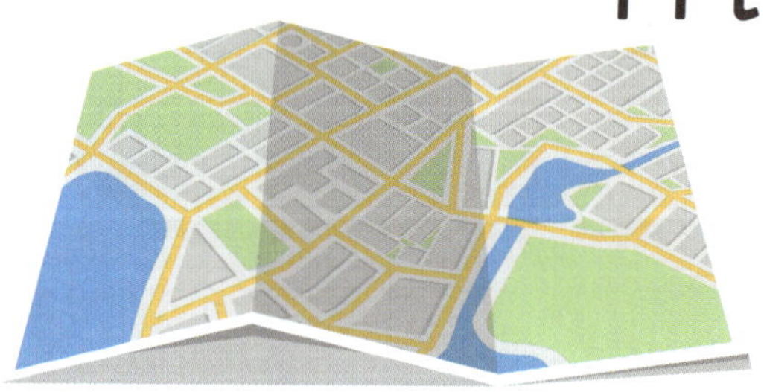

burn 

 prince

Write over and copy the letters.

v w

x z

Find and circle the letters **v**, **w**, **x** and **z** in the words below.

vase 

zoo 

 wave

 box

Write over and copy the letters.

ch wa

wh ad

Write over and copy the letters and joins.

ch wa

wh ad

Starter check

1. Draw lines to match the capital letters to the lower-case letters. The first one has been done for you.

C	p
D	d
O	r
Q	o
E	q
F	c
L	x
Y	l
J	f
P	j
R	w
W	y
X	e

2. Write in the missing letters to complete the words.

_ i _

_ uac _

_ a _ er

_ ello _

3. Write over and copy the words.

Queen

Sarah

Amir

London

	Not sure	Working on it	Yes I can
I can form lower-case letters correctly			
I can fit my letters into a space			
I can make my letters an even size			

ai ay

Challenge 1

Write over and copy the letters.

ai ai ai ___

ay ay ay ___

Circle **ai** or **ay** in the words below.

May

plain

grain

bay

hay

trail

Challenge 2

Write over and copy the letters and joins.

ai ai ai ______

ay ay ay ______

Challenge 3

Use the pictures to help you write **ai** or **ay** to complete the words.
Remember to join the missing letters.

tr _ _ n

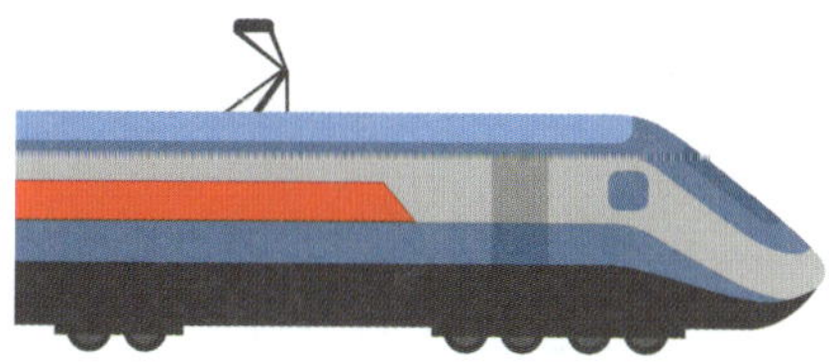

pl _ _

r _ _ n

Had a go ☐ Getting there ☐ Got it! ☐

ie ue ae

Challenge 1

Write over and copy the letters.

ie ie ie

ue ue ue

ae ae ae

Challenge 2

Write over and copy the letters and joins.

ie ie ie

ue ue ue

ae ae ae

Challenge 3

Write over and copy the sentences.

The aeroplane

T

flies in the blue sky.

f

Maisie queued for an

M

ice-cream sundae.

i

Had a go ☐ Getting there ☐ Got it! ☐

ir ar ur

Challenge 1

Write over and copy the letters.

ir ir ir

ar ar ar

ur ur ur

Challenge 2

Write over and copy the letters and joins.

ir ir ir

ar ar ar

ur ur ur

Challenge 3

Use the pictures to help you write **ir**, **ar** or **ur** to complete the words. Remember to join the missing letters.

squ _ _ rel

c _ _

h _ _ t

g _ _ l

Had a go ☐ Getting there ☐ Got it! ☐

ch th

Challenge 1

Write over and copy the letters.

ch ch ch

th th th

Challenge 2

Write over and copy the letters and joins.

ch ch ch

th th th

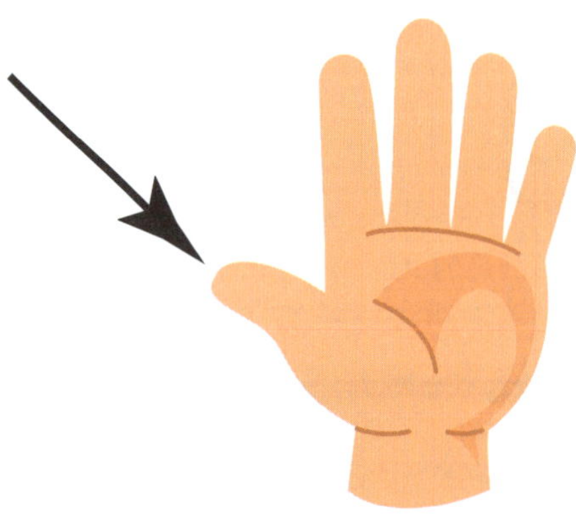

Challenge 3

Write over and copy the sentences.

She bit each peach

S

with her teeth.

w

The teacher told the

T

children to wear coats

c

in the chilly weather.

i

Had a go ☐ Getting there ☐ Got it! ☐

al all alk

Challenge 1

Write over and copy the letters.

al al al

all all all

alk alk alk

Challenge 2

Write over and copy the letters and joins.

al al al

all all all

alk alk alk

Challenge 3

Use the pictures to help you write **al**, **all** or **alk** to complete the words.
Remember to join the missing letters.

w_ _ _

b_ _ _oon

anim_ _

f_ _ _

Had a go ☐ Getting there ☐ Got it! ☐

oa ow ou

Challenge 1

Write over and copy the letters.

oa oa oa

ow ow ow

ou ou ou

Challenge 2

Write over and copy the letters and joins.

oa oa oa

ow ow ow

ou ou ou

Challenge 3

Write over and copy the sentence.

If you go out when

the wind blows, you

will need a coat.

Had a go ☐ Getting there ☐ Got it! ☐

we oe ve

Challenge 1

Write over and copy the letters.

we we we

oe oe oe

ve ve ve

Challenge 2

Write over and copy the letters and joins.

we we we

oe oe oe

ve ve ve

Challenge 3

Use the pictures to help you write **we**, **oe** or **ve** to complete the words.
Remember to join the missing letters.

_ _ t

sh _ _

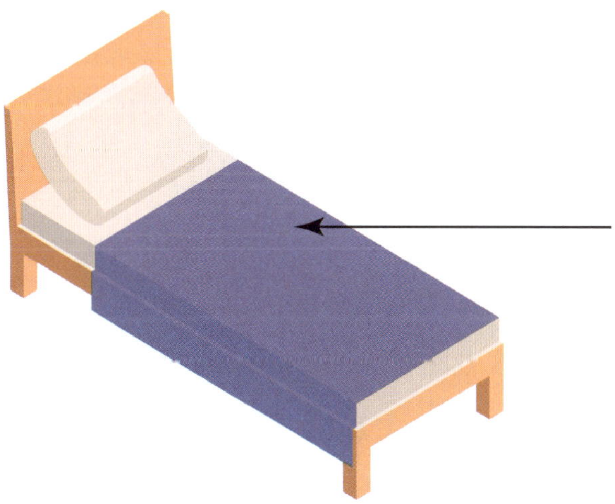

co _ _ r

ca _ _

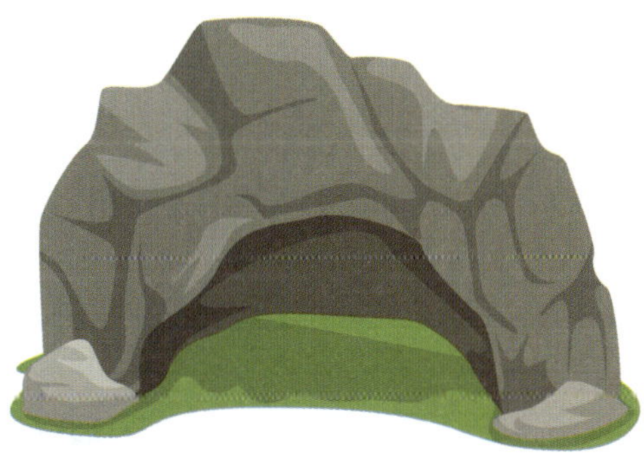

Had a go ☐ Getting there ☐ Got it! ☐

wh oh ot

Challenge 1

Write over and copy the letters.

wh wh wh

oh oh oh

ot ot ot

Challenge 2

Write over and copy the letters and joins.

wh wh wh

oh oh oh

ot ot ot

Challenge 3

Write over and copy the sentences.

John shouted, "Oh dear,

J

what are you doing?"

w

Mr Potts went

M

whale watching.

w

Had a go ☐ Getting there ☐ Got it! ☐

Progress check 1

1. Write over the letters and joins.

ai ie ar

ch all ur

we ay th

2. Write over the letters and then copy them using joins.

ai ______ ie ______ ar ______

ch ______ all ______ ur ______

we ______ ay ______ th ______

3. Copy the words.

snail

pie

furry

church

car

ball

4. Write over and copy the sentence.

Suram played catch

S

and then hurried home

a

for a bath.

f

Progress check 1

5. Write over and copy the letters and joins.

al ______ ow ______

ve ______ wh ______

6. Copy the words and joins.

animal

otter

beehive

whisker

crow

wheel

seal

7. Write over and copy the sentences.

The ball went in the

T

goal. "How was that?"

g

shouted the girl.

s

	Not sure	Working on it	Yes I can
I can make diagonal joins between short and tall letters			
I can copy horizontal joins between short and tall letters			
I can make the space between joined letters consistent			

Numbers 1–100

Challenge 1

Write over and copy the numbers.

1 1 1 ______

13 13 13 ______

53 53 53 ______

75 75 75 ______

89 89 89 ______

100 100 100 ______

Challenge 2

Write over and copy the number sequences.

0 ______ 2 ______ 4 ______ 6 ______

11 ______ 13 ______ 15 ______ 17 ______

Challenge 3

Write over and fill in the missing numbers to complete the sequences.

34 ____ 36 ____ 38 ____

91 ____ ____ 94 ____ 96

17 ____ 19 ____ ____ 22

Write the following numbers in the correct order.

13 20 55

95 72 30

6 17 4 10

4

Had a go ☐ Getting there ☐ Got it! ☐

Capital letters

Challenge 1

Write over each capital letter and write the lower-case letter next to it.

A B C D

E F G H

I J K L

M N O P

Q R S T

U V W X

Y Z

Challenge 2

Write over and copy the titles.

Mr ________ Mrs ________

Miss ________ Ms ________

Challenge 3

Write your name. Remember the capital letters.

Write the name of your teacher. Remember the capital letters.

Copy the names, correcting the capital letters in them.

mr patel

ms clegg

dr foster

Had a go ☐ Getting there ☐ Got it! ☐

ice ace ce

Challenge 1

Write over and copy the letters and joins.

ice ice ice

ace ace ace

ce ce ce

Challenge 2

Use the pictures to help you write **ice**, **ace** or **ce** to complete the words.

Remember to join the missing letters.

d _ _ _

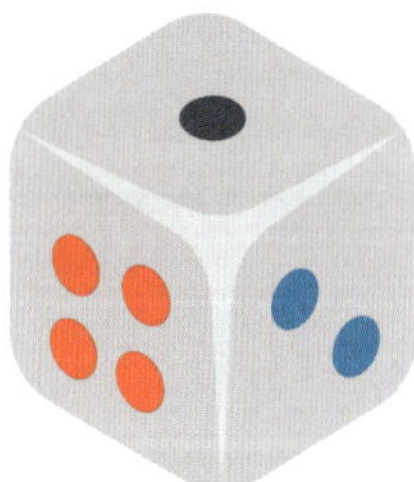

ra _ _

pal _ _ _

Challenge 3

Write over and copy the sentences.

The police officer had

T

a nice face.

a

Cinderella danced with

C

the prince at the palace.

t

Had a go ☐ Getting there ☐ Got it! ☐

ea ad

Challenge 1

Write over and copy the letters and joins.

ea ea ea ________

ad ad ad ________

Challenge 2

Use the pictures to help you write **ea** or **ad** to complete the words.

Remember to join the missing letters.

t _ _ m

s _ _

b _ _ r

ro _ _

Challenge 3

Write over and copy the sentence.

Brad and his dad had

B

fun at the seaside and

f

on the beach.

o

Had a go ☐ Getting there ☐ Got it! ☐

dg ng

Challenge 1

Write over and copy the letters and joins.

dg dg dg

ng ng ng

Challenge 2

Write over and copy the words and joins.

ring

hedge

finger

porridge

fridge

wing

Challenge 3

Write over and copy the sentences.

He dropped the ring

H

from the bridge.

f

I made some orange

I

fudge for Mrs Singh.

f

Had a go ☐ Getting there ☐ Got it! ☐

igh ing

Challenge 1

Write over and copy the letters and joins.

igh igh igh ______

ing ing ing ______

Challenge 2

Use the pictures to help you write **igh** or **ing** to complete the words. Remember to join the missing letters.

kn _ _ _ t

danc _ _ _

sle___ ___ ___

r___ ___ ___

Challenge 3

Write over and copy the sentence.

The wind is blowing and

T

the kite is flying high.

t

Had a go ☐ Getting there ☐ Got it! ☐

ee ea ey

Challenge 1

Write over and copy the letters and joins.

ee ee ee

ea ea ea

ey ey ey

Challenge 2

Use the pictures to help you write **ee**, **ea** or **ey** to complete the words.
Remember to join the missing letters.

mon__ __

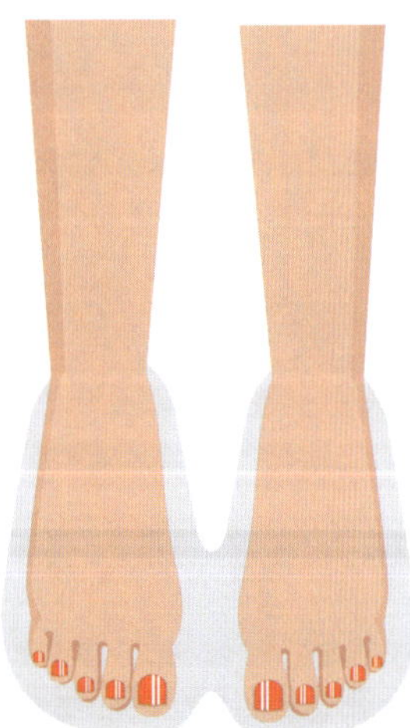

f__ __t

__ __rth

k__ __

Challenge 3

Write over and copy the sentence.

The bear eats all the

T

honey made by

h

the bees.

t

Had a go ☐ Getting there ☐ Got it! ☐

oo oa

Challenge 1

Write over and copy the letters and joins.

oo oo oo

oa oa oa

Challenge 2

Use the pictures to help you write **oo** or **oa** to complete the words.
Remember to join the missing letters.

g _ _ t

f _ _ d

Challenge 3

Write over and copy the sentences.

The boat will sail soon.

T

The toad jumped

T

across the road to get

a

to the cool pond.

t

Had a go ☐ Getting there ☐ Got it! ☐

Progress check 2

1. Write over and copy the numbers.

27 27 27 ________

19 19 19 ________

56 56 56 ________

44 44 44 ________

81 81 81 ________

37 37 37 ________

2. Write the missing letters in the words. Remember to join the missing letters.

i _ _ berg

s _ _ _ er

bri _ _ e

lo _ _

b _ _ k

3. Copy the words. Remember to add the joins that you know.

ring

bead

night

ice

lace

sleep

Progress check 2

4. Copy the words.

badge

wing

flight

thing

feet

steam

food

road

shoe

walk

5. Use the pictures to help you complete the words. Remember to join the missing letters.

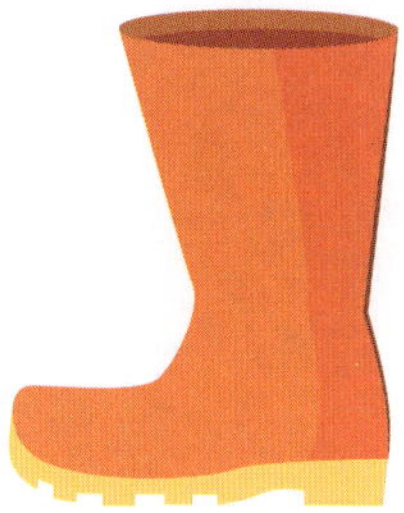

b _ _ t

c _ _ t

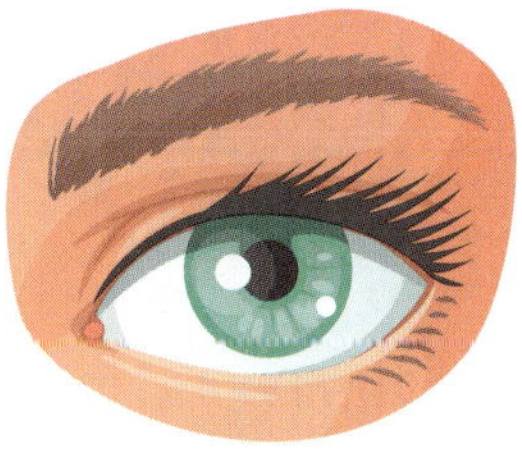

_ _ e

tr _ _

6. Copy the sentence. Remember to add the joins that you know.

Bees make nice honey.

B

	Not sure	Working on it	Yes I can
I can make diagonal joins to round letters			
I can join e and o in most words			
I can write capital letters at the right height and at the start of a word			

wa wo vi

Challenge 1

Write over and copy the letters and joins.

wa wa wa ________

wo wo wo ________

vi vi vi ________

Challenge 2

Use the pictures to help you write **wa**, **wo** or **vi** to complete the words.
Remember to join the missing letters.

___tch

___rk

___per

Challenge 3

Write over and copy the sentences.

The worm waited

T

by the violet flower.

b

We watched the

W

woman play the violin.

w

Had a go ☐ Getting there ☐ Got it! ☐

or aw au

Challenge 1

Write over and copy the letters and joins.

or or or

aw aw aw

au au au

Challenge 2

Use the pictures to help you write **or**, **aw** or **au** to complete the words. Remember to join the missing letters.

do __ __

p __ __

l __ __ gh

cr __ __ l

Challenge 3

Write over and copy the sentence.

My aunt won lots of

M

awards for sport.

a

Had a go ☐ Getting there ☐ Got it! ☐

an mb wr wh

Challenge 1

Write over and copy the letters and joins.

an an an ______

mb mb mb ______

wr wr wr ______

wh wh wh ______

Challenge 2

Use the pictures to help you write **an**, **mb**, **wr** or **wh** to complete the words. Remember to join the missing letters.

__ __ ite

s __ __ d

Challenge 3

Copy the sentences.

The lamb climbed

T

over the wrong wall.

o

My thumb is where?

M

It is on my hand.

I

Had a go ☐ Getting there ☐ Got it! ☐

ily ely ly

Challenge 1

Write over and copy the letters and joins.

ily ily ily ______

ely ely ely ______

ly ly ly ______

Challenge 2

Use the pictures to help you write **ily** or **ely** to complete the words.

Remember to join the missing letters.

lon___

l___

Challenge 3

Copy the sentences.

Amir sent some lovely

A

flowers to his Mum.

f

We safely held the

W

lively puppy.

l

Had a go ☐ Getting there ☐ Got it! ☐

kly kle

Challenge 1

Write over and copy the letters and joins.

kly kly kly ________

kle kle kle ________

Challenge 2

Use the pictures to help you write **kly** or **kle** to complete the words.
Remember to join the missing letters.

quic _ _ _

an _ _ _

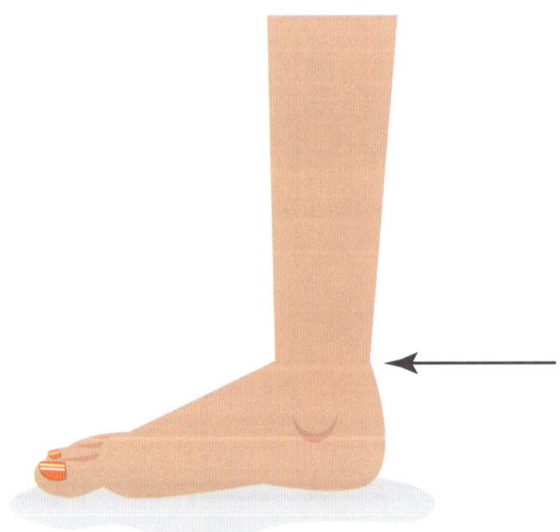

Challenge 3

Copy the sentences.

The ring sparkled in

T

the moonlight.

t

The sweets were too

T

sickly.

s

Had a go ☐ Getting there ☐ Got it! ☐

# of ful to at

Challenge 1

Write over and copy the letters and joins.

of of of ______

ful ful ful ______

to to to ______

at at at ______

Challenge 2

Use the pictures to help you write **of**, **ful**, **to** or **at** to complete the words.
Remember to join the missing letters.

__ __ ast

g __ __ e

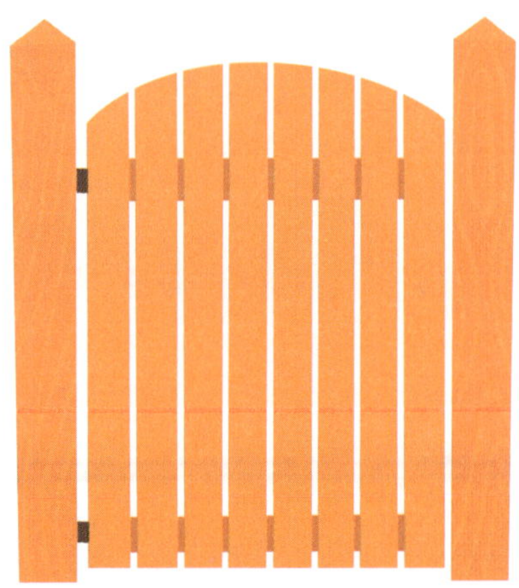

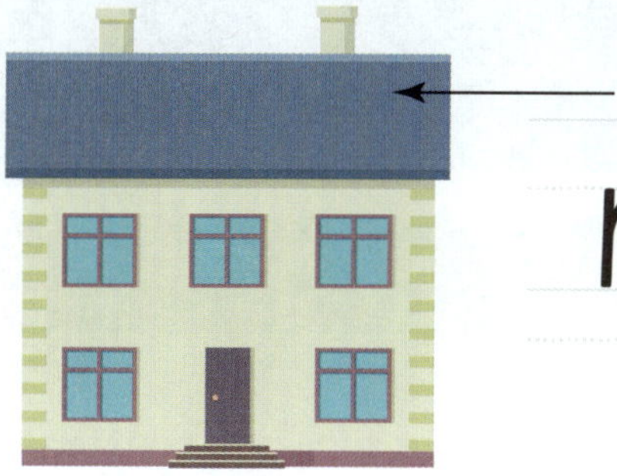

ro _ _

_ _ _ l

Challenge 3

Write over and copy the sentence.

Mrs Platt told the boy

M

to be careful.

t

Had a go ☐ Getting there ☐ Got it! ☐

ui ey aw ur an ip

Challenge 1

Write over and copy the letters and joins.

ui ui ui ________

ey ey ey ________

aw aw aw ________

ur ur ur ________

an an an ________

ip ip ip ________

Challenge 2

Use the pictures to help you write **ui**, **ey**, **aw**, **ur**, **an** or **ip** to complete the words. Remember to join the missing letters.

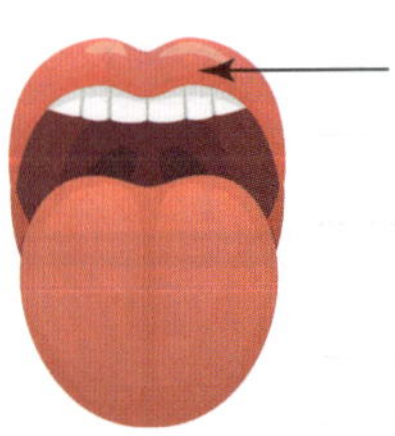

l __ __ s

hon __ __

cr _ _ l

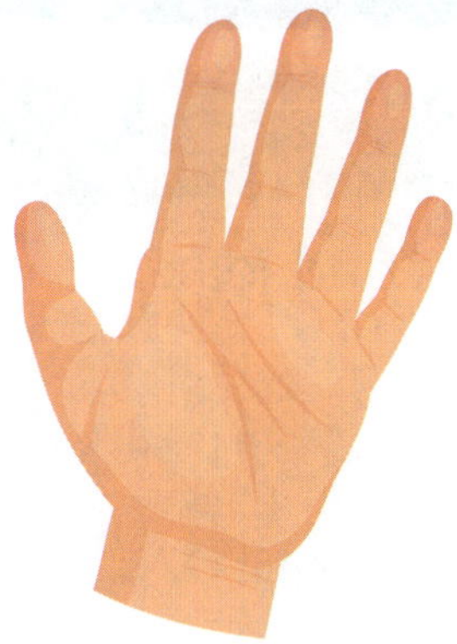

h _ _ d

Challenge 3

Write over and copy the sentence.

Turn the grey key and

T

open the door to the

o

building.

b

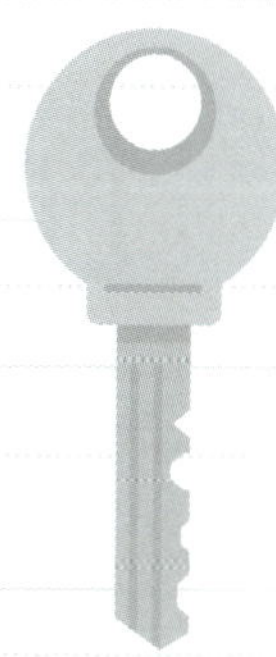

Had a go ☐ Getting there ☐ Got it! ☐

ck al el at il

Challenge 1

Write over and copy the letters and joins.

ck ck ck ______

al al al ______

el el el ______

at at at ______

il il il ______

Challenge 2

Use the pictures to help you write **ck**, **al**, **el**, **at** or **il** to complete the words.
Remember to join the missing letters.

tru _ _

c _ _

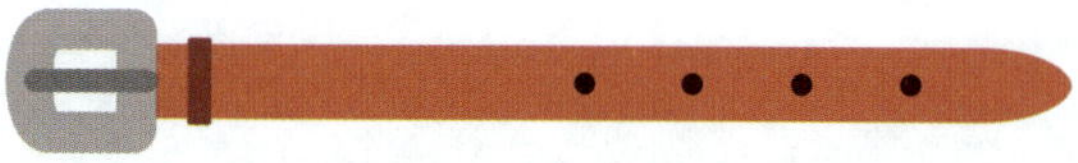

b __ __ t

h __ __ l

Challenge 3

Write over and copy the sentence.

The magician, called

T

Billy, wore a tall hat as

B

he performed his trick.

h

Had a go ☐ Getting there ☐ Got it! ☐

ai ay on op ov

Challenge 1

Write over and copy the letters and joins.

ai ai ai ______

ay ay ay ______

on on on ______

op op op ______

ov ov ov ______

Challenge 2

Use the pictures to help you write **ai**, **ay**, **on**, **op**, or **ov** to complete the words. Remember to join the missing letters.

tr __ __ n

sh __ __

gl __ __ es

cr __ __ on

Challenge 3

Write over and copy the sentence.

The paint shop is on

T

the way to the main

t

street.

s

Had a go ☐ Getting there ☐ Got it! ☐

Progress check 3

1. Copy the words using the joins that you know.

watch

violin

woman

2. Use the pictures to help you complete the words. Remember to join the missing letters where necessary. Then copy the full word.

d ___ ___ ___

p ___ ___

___ ___ ong

c ___ ___ ___

3. Copy the sentences. Remember to add the joins you know.

The lively lambs are

T

eating the straw. How

e

naughty they are!

n

The girl quickly

T

ran home.

r

Progress check 3

4. Copy the words using the joins that you know.

joyful

catch

tomato

5. Use the pictures to help you complete the words. Remember to join the missing letters where necessary. Then copy the full word.

g ___ ___ l

h ___ ___ ___

l ___ ___ e

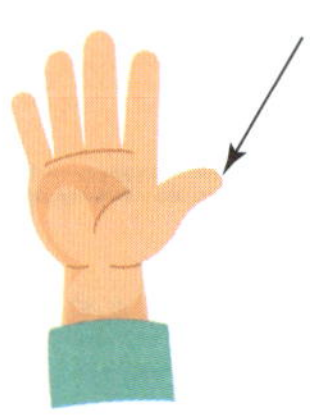

t ___ ___ ___ ___

6. Copy the sentence. Remember to add the joins you know.

“Yuck,” said Ahmed,

Y

“that cake made me

t

feel ill!”

f

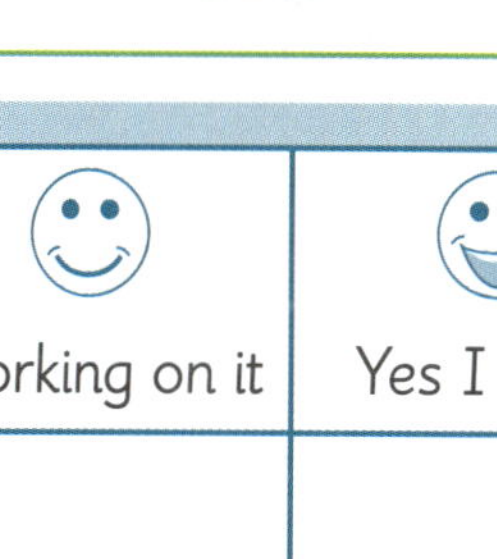

	Not sure	Working on it	Yes I can
I get the right space between two letters			
I can write capital letters at the start of names and places			
I can copy printed words adding the joins that I know			

ol op ob ot

Challenge 1

Write over and copy the letters and joins.

ol ol ol

op op op

ob ob ob

ot ot ot

Challenge 2

Use the pictures to help you write **ol**, **op**, **ob**, or **ot** to complete the words. Remember to join the missing letters.

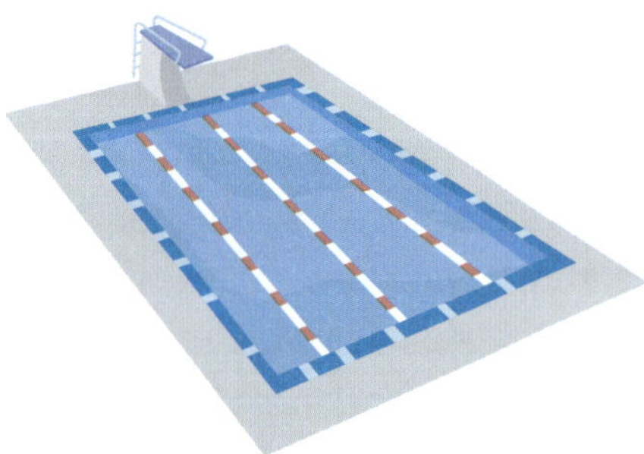

po__ __

h__ __

r __ __ in

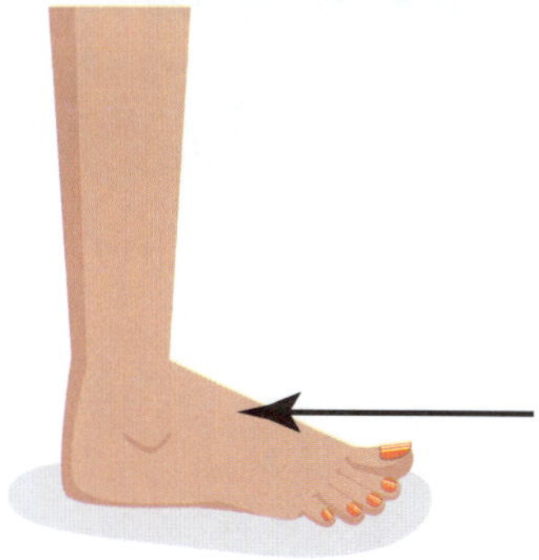

fo __ __

Challenge 3

Write over and copy the sentence.

The school is not open

T

today.

t

Had a go ☐ Getting there ☐ Got it! ☐

ed cc eg ic ad ug dd ag

Challenge 1

Write over the letters and practise the joins.

ed ed ed

cc cc cc

eg eg eg

ic ic ic

ad ad ad

ug ug ug

dd dd dd

ag ag ag

Challenge 2

Use the pictures to help you write **ed**, **cc**, **eg**, **ic**, **ad**, **ug**, **dd** or **ag** to complete the words. Remember to join the missing letters.

b __ __

com __ __

__ __ g

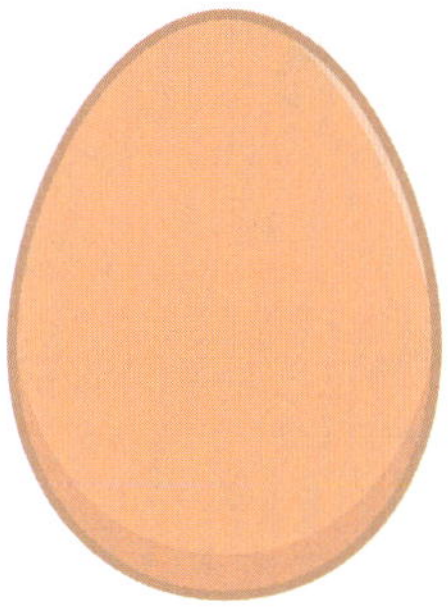

m __ __

Challenge 3

Write over and copy the sentence.

His daddy agreed to

H

let him go ice-skating.

l

Had a go ☐ Getting there ☐ Got it! ☐

oc og od va vo

Challenge 1

Write over and copy the letters and joins.

oc oc oc ______

og og og ______

od od od ______

va va va ______

vo vo vo ______

Challenge 2

Use the pictures to help you write **oc**, **og**, **od**, **va** or **vo** to complete the words.
Remember to join the missing letters.

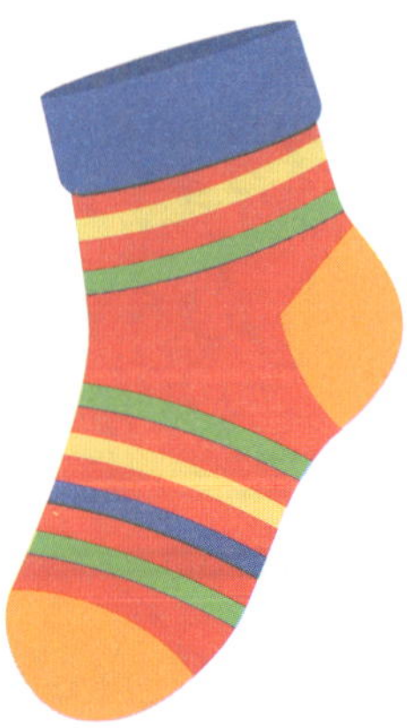

s _ _ k

d _ _

n

fo

Challenge 3

Write over and copy the sentence.

The dog food vanished

T

quickly.

q

Had a go ☐ Getting there ☐ Got it! ☐

Capital letters and alphabetic sequence

Challenge 1

Add the missing capital letters to complete the alphabet.

A B ___ ___ E

F G ___ ___ ___

K ___ M ___ O

P Q R S T

___ ___ ___ X

___ Z

Challenge 2

Write these words in alphabetical order.

apple

banana

orange

Challenge 3

Draw lines to match the lower-case letters to the capital letters. The first one has been done for you.

d	Z
a	F
f	K
g	D
v	J
z	A
e	G
j	E
k	V

Had a go ☐ Getting there ☐ Got it! ☐

Capital letters for names

Challenge 1

Copy the names. Add the capital letters in the correct places.

mrs jones

mr williams

miss kumar

Challenge 2

Copy each row of names in alphabetical order. Add the capital letters in the correct places.

ranjit charlie sid

melissa lara daniel

Challenge 3

Copy the sentences. Remember to start the names with a capital letter.

mark bought a book.

yusuf played golf.

alisha sang songs.

Had a go ☐ Getting there ☐ Got it! ☐

Capital letters for placenames

Challenge 1

Copy the placenames. Add the capital letters at the beginning of the names.

cardiff

paris

madrid

new york

london

glasgow

Challenge 2

Copy each row of placenames in alphabetical order. Add the capital letters in the correct place.

alford skegness elstree

tetney york wilmslow

Challenge 3

Write your own placenames in the spaces. Remember to start the placenames with a capital letter. Then copy the completed sentences.

I live in ____________________.

My school is called

____

____________________.

Had a go ☐ Getting there ☐ Got it! ☐

Correct spacing

Challenge 1

Copy the names.

Susan

Jupiter

Atlantic

Sahara

John

Challenge 2

Draw lines to show where there should be spaces between the words in the sentence.

InAutumntheleaves

fall,turninggolden

brownandorange.

Challenge 3

There are no spaces between the words in this poem. Copy the poem, adding spaces between the words. Check your spacing between letters and words is correct.

Springbringsdaffodils

S

Blowinginthebreeze

B

Yellow,whiteandgold.

Y

Had a go ☐ Getting there ☐ Got it! ☐

Alphabetical order

Challenge 1

Write the words on the shopping list in an alphabetical list.

sugar tomatoes
flour eggs

Challenge 2

Write the words in alphabetical order.

bird goat ant horse

Challenge 3

Write your first name and then rearrange the letters in alphabetical order.

Write the name of the town where you live and then rearrange the letters in alphabetical order.

Had a go ☐ Getting there ☐ Got it! ☐

Progress check 4

1. Copy the words.

olive

bridge

robot

other

lock

object

shed

2. Use the pictures to help you complete the words. Remember to join the missing letters.

 b___ ___

 l___ ___ ___ ___ ___

j___ ___ ___

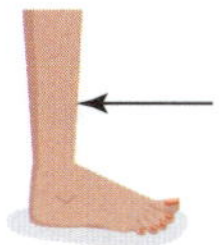

l___ ___

3. Copy the sentences. Use the joins you know.

The doctor's dog has vanished!

The dog is black and his name is Ned.

Progress check 4

4. Copy the words and names. Add capital letters where they are needed.

hiccup

admit

mrs adams

the river thames

mr thomson

fog

5. Copy the sentence. Check your spacing between letters and words is correct.

The Great Fire of

London started in 1666.

	Not sure	Working on it	Yes I can
I get the right space between words			
I can write clear capitals at the start of proper nouns			
I can join to round letters			
I can make an alphabetical list			

Progress chart

Draw ticks in the boxes to show how you feel about your handwriting.

	Not sure	Working on it	Yes I can!
I can make diagonal joins between short and tall letters			
I can copy horizontal joins between short and tall letters			
I can make the space between joined letters consistent			
I can make diagonal joins to round letters			
I can join **e** and **o** in most words			
I can write capital letters at the right height and at the start of a word			
I get the right space between two letters			
I can write capital letters at the start of names and places			
I can copy printed words adding the joins that I know.			
I get the right space between words			
I can write clear capitals at the start of proper nouns			
I can join to round letters			
I can make an alphabetical list			